PRAYER JOURNAL

THE POWER OF A
PRAYING®
PARENT

Reflections from
Stormie Omartian

HARVEST HOUSE PUBLISHERS
Eugene, Oregon 97402

Cover by Koechel Peterson & Associates, Minneapolis, Minnesota

THE POWER OF A PRAYING® PARENT PRAYER JOURNAL

Copyright © 2002 by Stormie Omartian
Published by Harvest House Publishers
Eugene, Oregon 97402

ISBN 0-7369-0917-6

Printed in the United States of America

02 03 04 05 06 07 / DC-MS / 10 9 8 7 6 5 4 3 2 1

June 15, 05

Welcome
to a life of prayer...

One of the most powerful things you can do for your children is to pray for them. The next most powerful thing would be to record those prayers in a book, such as this, so you can refer to them again and again. Then someday in the not-too-distant future, you can look back on them and see how the Lord answered. If you were so inclined, it could also be a wonderful book for your children to read one day when they are old enough to appreciate the significance of your prayers over their lives. What a great faith-builder it is for a son or daughter to know that their mother or father prayed for them and to see how God answered those prayers.

With all that said, don't let the idea of possibly show-ing what you have written on these pages put pressure on you to try and make your thoughts and words perfect. Just write out the cries of your heart for your children, and for yourself as a parent, openly and honestly before the Lord. Share all your thoughts, fears, feelings, hopes, dreams, concerns, and prayer requests. Putting those things down on paper will help you crystallize what you are sensing about each child and what you hope for each of their lives. I pray that the scriptures and short prayers I have included here will be an inspiration to you to go into more detail about the specific issues that you and your children face. If one day in the future you want to share all this with your children you can. Until then, this is between you and God.

—STORMIE OMARTIAN

You did not choose Me, but I chose you and appointed you that you should go and bear fruit, and that your fruit should remain, that whatever you ask the Father in My name He may give you.

—JOHN 15:16

Lord, please help me to be a godly role model. Give me the communication, teaching, and nurturing skills that I must have. Make me the parent You want me to be, and teach me how to pray and truly intercede for the life of this child. Lord, You said in Your Word, "Whatever things you ask in prayer, believing, you will receive" (Matthew 21:22). In Jesus' name I ask that You will increase my faith to believe for all the things You've put on my heart to pray for concerning this child.

Abby—

June 15, 2005

Lord I pray that she would have a joyful spirit and true Love for Life and you! Let her mind and heart be ruled by your word. Do not let her stray from you. ditto 9-25-07
Jnr. High

I pray she will go to horse camp because she said she would. Keep her safe there. (She did go, and she Loved it)

Joe—

Lord grow him into the Knight you envision him to be. Cover him w/ your gentle strength and courage. Help him not to have nightmares and help him to run from the sources of nightmares. Game cube, scary movies etc.

Keep Joe safe at horse camp if he goes.
(He went and it was okay, Long day) too little

Dear Lord, Abby is 11 and has started jnr high at Fisher middle school. Let your word come to the surface of her heart and reflect in her talk and actions. Be with her in the difficult choices. I need to let her make some choices, be there when she needs it. Give Kevin & I wisdom.

9-27-07

well it is Jan. 29th 2008, Abby is doing well on the ~~inside~~ outside:
- very cute
- straght A's second quarter :)
- good athlete

not sure about her insides
- her compassionate heart
- her ability to see the humor
- her Kindness quotient
- her Longing for Your word and Your instruction.

I'll catch up w/ You soon for a reflection

...teach me how to pray

Ask, and it will be given to you; seek, and you will find; knock, and it will be opened to you. For everyone who asks receives, and he who seeks finds, and to him who knocks it will be opened.

—MATTHEW 7:7-8

Lord, I want to partner with You and partake of Your gifts of wisdom, discernment, revelation, and guidance as I care for my child. I also need Your strength and patience, along with a generous portion of Your love flowing through me. Teach me how to love him (her) the way You love. Where I need to be healed, delivered, changed, matured, or made whole, I invite You to do that in me.

Ask, and it will be given to you; seek, and you will find; knock, and it will be opened to you. For Everyone who asks receives, and he who seeks finds, and to him who knocks it will be opened.

Matt 7: 7-8

Noble character: strength, ability efficiency, wealth, valor, enterprising, energetic, always occupied

Oct. 5, 2005
Hospitality - is placed between Hospice/Hospital in dictionary.
Hospice - shelter
Hospital - a place of healing

Lord, I pray that our home would be used for your purposes as a place of healing and a shelter.

Sept. 07   6th Grade

Lord, help me to give
Abby the right amount
of freedom to teach responsibleness
but not so much that
irrepairable damage can be
done. I need your
guidance here. Please
surround her with good
and wholesome friends.

2nd Grade - Joe

Lord, please let Joe have several good friends. Help Kevin and I parent him to be a "modern day night". LOVE that term:

Gentle
courage
confident
kind
considerate
able to where another's shoes

Amen.

They shall not labor in vain, nor bring forth children for trouble; for they shall be the descendants of the blessed of the LORD and their offspring with them.

—ISAIAH 65:23

Lord, You alone know what (name of child) needs. I release him (her) to You to care for and protect, and I commit myself to pray for everything concerning him (her) that I can think of or that You put upon my heart. Teach me how to pray and guide me in what to pray about. Help me not to impose my *own* will when I'm praying for him (her), but rather enable me to pray that *Your* will be done in his (her) life.

Prayer Journal

_____
_____
_____
_____
_____
_____
_____
_____
_____
_____
_____
_____
_____
_____
_____
_____
_____
_____
_____
_____
_____
_____
_____
_____
_____
_____

...I commit myself to pray

Whatever we ask we receive from Him,
because we keep His commandments and do
those things that are pleasing in His sight.

—1 JOHN 3:22

Lord, I know that You have given (name
of child) to me to care for and raise.
Help me to do that. Show me places
where I continue to hang on to him (her)
and enable me to release him (her) to
Your protection, guidance, and counsel.
Help me not to live in fear of possible
dangers, but in the joy and peace of
knowing that You are in control.

Prayer Journal

Prayer Journal

_____

_____

_____

_____

_____

_____

_____

_____

_____

_____

_____

_____

_____

_____

_____

_____

_____

_____

_____

_____

_____

_____

_____

_____

_____

_____

...You are in control

*I will both lie down in peace, and sleep; for
You alone, O LORD, make me dwell in safety.*

—PSALM 4:8

Lord, I ask that You would put a hedge of
protection around (name of child). Protect
her (his) spirit, body, mind, and emotions
from any kind of evil or harm. I pray specifically for protection from accidents, disease,
injury, or any other physical, mental, or
emotional abuse. I pray that she (he) will
make her (his) refuge "in the shadow of
Your wings...until these calamities have
passed by" (Psalm 57:1).

Prayer Journal

Prayer Journal

...a hedge of protection

I have loved you with an everlasting love;
therefore with lovingkindness I have drawn
you.

—JEREMIAH 31:3

Lord, help (name of child) to abide in
Your love. May he (she) say as David did,
"Cause me to hear Your lovingkindness in
the morning, for in You do I trust" (Psalm
143:8). Manifest Your love to this child in
a real way today and help him (her) to
receive it.

Prayer Journal

Since you have purified your souls in obeying the truth through the Spirit in sincere love of the brethren, love one another fervently with a pure heart.

—1 PETER 1:22-23

Lord, as (name of child) grows in the confidence of being loved and accepted, release in him (her) the capacity to easily *communicate* love to others. As he (she) comes to fully understand the depth of Your love for him (her) and receives it into his (her) soul, make him (her) a vessel through which Your love flows to others. In Jesus' name I pray.

Prayer Journal

For this is good and acceptable in the sight of God our Savior, who desires all men to be saved and to come to the knowledge of the truth.

—1 TIMOTHY 2:3-4

Lord, You have said in Your Word, "If you confess with your mouth the Lord Jesus and believe in your heart that God has raised Him from the dead, you will be saved" (Romans 10:9). I pray for that kind of faith for my child. May she (he) call You her (his) Savior, be filled with Your Holy Spirit, acknowledge You in every area of her (his) life, and choose always to follow You and Your ways.

Prayer Journal

Prayer Journal

...choose to follow You

We know that the Son of God has come and has given us an understanding, that we may know Him who is true; and we are in Him who is true, in His Son Jesus Christ. This is the true God and eternal life.

1 JOHN 5:20

Lord, may (name of child) always know Your will, have spiritual understanding, and walk in a manner that is pleasing in Your sight. You have said in Your Word that You will pour out Your Spirit on my offspring (Isaiah 44:3). I pray that You would pour out Your Spirit upon (name of child) this day. Open her (his) heart and bring her (him) to a full knowledge of the truth about You.

Prayer Journal

Prayer Journal

...full knowledge of the truth

Correct your son and he will give you rest.

—PROVERBS 29:17

Lord, turn my child's heart toward You so that all he (she) does is pleasing in Your sight. May he (she) learn to identify and confront pride and rebellion in himself (herself) and be willing to confess and repent of it. Make him (her) uncomfortable with sin. Help him (her) to know the beauty and simplicity of walking with a sweet and humble spirit in obedience and submission to You.

Prayer Journal

_____
_____
_____
_____
_____
_____
_____
_____
_____
_____
_____
_____
_____
_____
_____
_____
_____
_____
_____
_____
_____
_____
_____
_____
_____
_____
_____

_____
_____
_____
_____
_____
_____
_____
_____
_____
_____
_____
_____
_____
_____
_____
_____
_____
_____
_____
_____
_____
_____
_____
_____
_____

Prayer Journal

_...turn my child's heart
towards You_

Make Your face shine upon Your servant, and
teach me Your statutes.

—Psalm 119:135

Lord, put into (name of child) a longing to
spend time with You, in Your Word, and in
prayer, listening for Your voice. Shine Your
light upon any secret or unseen rebellion
that is taking root in his (her) heart so that
it can be identified and destroyed. Lord, I
pray that he (she) will not give himself (herself) over to pride, selfishness, and rebellion,
but that he (she) will be delivered from it.

Prayer Journal

Prayer Journal

...listening for Your voice

The love of God has been poured out in our
hearts by the Holy Spirit who was given to us.

—ROMANS 5:5

Lord, fill my child's heart with Your love
and give her (him) an abundance of compassion and forgiveness that will overflow to
each member of the family. Specifically, I
pray for a close, happy, loving, and fulfilling
relationship between (name of child) and
(name of family member) for all the days of
their lives. Help them to love, value, appreciate, and respect one another so that the
God-ordained tie between them cannot be
broken.

Prayer Journal

_____
_____
_____
_____
_____
_____
_____
_____
_____
_____
_____
_____
_____
_____
_____
_____
_____
_____
_____
_____
_____
_____
_____
_____
_____

*...fill my child's heart
with Your love*

Now I plead with you, brethren, by the name of our Lord Jesus Christ, that you all speak the same thing, and that there be no divisions among you, but that you be perfectly joined together in the same mind and in the same judgment.

—1 CORINTHIANS 1:10

Lord, Your Word instructs us to "be of one mind, having compassion for one another; love as brothers, be tenderhearted, be courteous" (1 Peter 3:8). Help (name of child) to live accordingly, "endeavoring to keep the unity of the Spirit in the bond of peace" (Ephesians 4:3). In Jesus' name I pray that You would instill a love and compassion in her (him) for all family members that is strong and unending.

Prayer Journal

Prayer Journal

...the bond of peace

The righteous should choose his friends carefully.

—Proverbs 12:26

Lord, give (name of child) the wisdom he (she) needs to choose friends who are godly, and help him (her) to never compromise his (her) walk with You in order to gain acceptance. Give me Holy Spirit-inspired discernment in how I guide or influence him (her) in the selection of friends. I pray that You would take anyone who is *not* a godly influence *out* of his (her) life or else transform that person into Your likeness.

Prayer Journal

...provide godly friends

As one whom his mother comforts, so I will comfort you.

—Isaiah 66:13

Lord, whenever my child experiences grief over a lost friendship, comfort him (her) and send new friends with whom he (she) can connect, share, and be the person You created him (her) to be. Take away any loneliness or low self-esteem that would cause him (her) to seek out less than God-glorifying relationships. I pray that You would teach him (her) the meaning of true friendship.

Prayer Journal

Prayer Journal

...send new friends

Teach me Your way, O LORD; I will walk in
Your truth; unite my heart to fear Your name.
I will praise You, O Lord my God, with all
my heart, and I will glorify Your name
forevermore.

—PSALM 86:11–12

Lord, give (name of child) a desire for the
truth of Your Word and a love for Your
laws and Your ways. May she (he) be so
aware of the fullness of Your Holy Spirit in
her (him) that when she (he) is depleted in
any way she (he) will immediately run to
You to be renewed and refreshed. May a
deep reverence and love for You and Your
ways color everything she (he) does and
every choice she (he) makes.

Prayer Journal

...deep reverence and love for You

Give me understanding, and I shall keep Your law; indeed, I shall observe it with my whole heart.

—PSALM 119:34

Lord, please strengthen (name of child) to stand strong in her (his) convictions. As she (he) learns to read Your Word, write Your law in her (his) mind and on her (his) heart so that she (he) always walks with a confident assurance of the righteousness of Your commands. As she (he) learns to pray, may she (he) also learn to listen for Your voice.

Prayer Journal

Prayer Journal

...listen for Your voice

*You are a chosen generation, a royal priest-
hood, a holy nation, His own special people,
that you may proclaim the praises of Him
who called you out of darkness into His mar-
velous light.*

—1 PETER 2:9

Lord, I pray (name of child) will be a leader
of people into Your kingdom. Help him
(her) to grow into a complete understanding
of his (her) authority in Jesus while retain-
ing a submissive and humble spirit. May the
fruit of the Spirit, which is love, joy, peace,
patience, kindness, goodness, faithfulness,
gentleness, and self-control, grow in him
(her) daily (Galatians 5:22-23).

Prayer Journal

_____
_____
_____
_____
_____
_____
_____
_____
_____
_____
_____
_____
_____
_____
_____
_____
_____
_____
_____
_____
_____
_____
_____
_____

We know that all things work together for good to those who love God, to those who are the called according to His purpose.

—ROMANS 8:28

Lord, please give (name of child) a vision for his (her) life when setting goals for the future and a sense of purpose about what You've called him (her) to do. Help him (her) to see himself (herself) as You do— from his (her) future and not from his (her) past. I pray that You would pour out Your Spirit upon (name of child) this day and anoint him (her) for all that You've called him (her) to be and do.

Prayer Journal

Prayer Journal

...pour out Your Spirit

I have chosen the way of truth; Your judgments I have laid before me.

—PSALM 119:30

Lord, please give (name of child) a heart that loves truth and follows after it. Your Word says that "when He, the Spirit of truth, has come, He will guide you into all truth" (John 16:13). I pray that Your Spirit of truth will guide (name of child) into all truth. May she (he) never be a person who gives place to lies, but rather a person of integrity who follows hard after the Spirit of truth.

...*He will guide you into all truth*

Your light shall break forth like the morning,
your healing shall spring forth speedily, and
your righteousness shall go before you; the
glory of the LORD shall be your rear guard.

—ISAIAH 58:8

Lord, I pray that sickness and infirmity will have no place or power in my child's life. I pray for protection against any disease coming into his (her) body. Your Word says, "He sent His word and healed them, and delivered them from their destructions" (Psalm 107:20). I look to You for a life of health, healing, and wholeness for my child.

Prayer Journal

...health, healing, wholeness

Christ also suffered for us, leaving us an
example, that you should follow His steps...
who Himself bore our sins in His own body
on the tree, that we, having died to sins,
might live for righteousness—by whose stripes
you were healed.

—1 PETER 2:21,24

Lord, thank You that You suffered and died
for us so that we might be healed. I lay
claim to that heritage of healing that You
have promised in Your Word and provided
for those who believe. If part of that healing
means seeing a doctor, I pray that You,
Lord, would show us who that should be.
Give that doctor wisdom and full knowledge of the best way to proceed.

Prayer Journal

...that we might be healed

Do you not know that your body is the temple of the Holy Spirit who is in you, whom you have from God, and you are not your own? For you were bought at a price; therefore glorify God in your body and in your spirit, which are God's.

—1 CORINTHIANS 6:19-20

Lord, I pray that (name of child) will always have a desire to eat properly, and that You would also give her (him) the motivation to exercise regularly, to drink plenty of pure water, and to control and manage stress in her (his) life by living according to Your Word. Whenever she (he) struggles in any of those areas may she (he) turn to You and say, "Teach me Your way, O LORD" (Psalm 27:11).

Prayer Journal

...living according to Your Word

Do not let your adornment be merely out-
ward—arranging the hair, wearing gold, or
putting on fine apparel—rather let it be the
hidden person of the heart, with the incor-
ruptible beauty of a gentle and quiet spirit,
which is very precious in the sight of God.

—1 PETER 3:3-5

Lord, I pray that (name of child) will not be
bound by the lure of fashion magazines, tele-
vision, or movies which try to influence her
(him) with an image of what they say she
(he) should look like. Help her (him) to see
that what makes a person truly attractive is
Your Holy Spirit living in her (him) and
radiating outward. May she (he) come to
understand that true attractiveness begins in
the heart of one who loves God.

Prayer Journal

...the hidden person of the heart

*Let my cry come before You, O LORD; give
me understanding according to Your word.*

—PSALM 119:169

Lord, may (name of child) hide Your Word
in his (her) heart like a treasure, and seek
after understanding like silver or gold. Give
him (her) a good mind, a teachable spirit,
and an ability to learn. Instill in him (her) a
desire to attain knowledge and skill, and
may he (she) have *joy* in the process. Help
him (her) to excel in school and do well in
any classes he (she) may take.

Prayer Journal

...a teachable spirit

Show me Your ways, O LORD; *teach me Your paths. Lead me in Your truth and teach me, for You are the God of my salvation; on You I wait all the day.*

—PSALM 25:4-5

Lord, I pray that my child will be taught by You, for Your Word says that when our children are taught by You they are guaranteed peace. You have also said, "The fear of the LORD is the beginning of knowledge, but fools despise wisdom and instruction" (Proverbs 1:7). May he (she) never be a fool and turn away from learning, but rather may he (she) turn to You for the knowledge he (she) needs.

Prayer Journal

...lead my child in Your truth

As each one has received a gift, minister it to one another, as good stewards of the manifold grace of God.

—1 Peter 4:10

Lord, Your Word says, "Having then gifts differing according to the grace that is given to us, let us use them" (Romans 12:6). I pray You would develop the gifts and talents You have placed in (name of child) and use them for Your glory. Make them apparent to me and to her (him), and show me specifically if there is any special nurturing, training, learning experience, or opportunities I should provide for her (him).

Prayer Journal

…use them for Your glory

You have blessed the work of his hands, and
his possessions have increased in the land.

—JOB 1:10

Lord, bless the work of my child's hands,
and may she (he) be able to earn a good living doing the work she (he) loves and does
best. Your Word says that "a man's gift
makes room for him, and brings him before
great men" (Proverbs 18:16). May whatever
she (he) does find favor with others and be
well received and respected.

Prayer Journal

The Power of a Praying Parent

...earn a good living

Pleasant words are like a honeycomb, sweetness to the soul and health to the bones.

—PROVERBS 16:24

Lord, fill my child's heart with Your Spirit and Your truth so that what overflows from his (her) mouth will be words of life and not death. Put a monitor over his (her) mouth so that every temptation to use profane, negative, cruel, hurtful, uncaring, unloving, or compassionless language would pierce his (her) spirit and make him (her) feel uncomfortable. Enable him (her) to always speak words of hope, health, encouragement, and life.

Prayer Journal

_____
_____
_____
_____
_____
_____
_____
_____
_____
_____
_____
_____
_____
_____
_____
_____
_____
_____
_____
_____
_____
_____

How can a young man cleanse his way? By taking heed according to Your word. With my whole heart I have sought You; Oh, let me not wander from Your commandments! Your word I have hidden in my heart, that I might not sin against You!

—PSALM 119:9-11

Lord, hide Your Word in my child's heart so that there is no attraction to sin. I pray she (he) will run from evil, from impurity, from unholy thoughts, words, and deeds, and that she (he) will be drawn toward whatever is pure and holy. Let Christ be formed in her (him) and cause her (him) to seek the power of Your Holy Spirit to enable her (him) to do what is right.

Prayer Journal

*...with my whole heart
I have sought You*

Grant us that we...might serve Him without fear, in holiness and righteousness before Him all the days of our life.

—LUKE 1:74-75

Lord, may a desire for holiness that comes from a pure heart be reflected in all that my child does. Where she (he) has strayed from the path of holiness, bring her (him) to repentance and work Your cleansing power in her (his) heart and life. Give her (him) understanding that to live in purity brings wholeness and blessing, and that the greatest reward for it is seeing You.

Prayer Journal

_____
_____
_____
_____
_____
_____
_____
_____
_____
_____
_____
_____
_____
_____
_____
_____
_____
_____
_____
_____
_____
_____
_____
_____
_____
_____

...a desire for holiness

My people will dwell in a peaceful habitation,
in secure dwellings, and in quiet resting
places.

—ISAIAH 32:18

Lord, I pray over my child's room. Please
put Your complete protection over these
four walls so that evil cannot enter here by
any means. Fill this room with Your love,
peace, and joy. I pray that my child will say,
as David did, "I will walk within my house
with a perfect heart. I will set nothing
wicked before my eyes" (Psalm 101:2-3). I
pray that You, Lord, will make this room a
holy place, sanctified for Your glory.

Prayer Journal

_____

_____

_____

_____

_____

_____

_____

_____

_____

_____

_____

_____

_____

_____

_____

_____

_____

_____

_____

_____

_____

_____

_____

_____

_____

_____

_____

_____

..make this room a holy place

He shall cover you with His feathers, and under His wings you shall take refuge; His truth shall be your shield and buckler. You shall not be afraid of the terror by night, nor of the arrow that flies by day, nor of the pestilence that walks in darkness, nor of the destruction that lays waste at noonday.

—PSALM 91:4-6

Lord, You said You have "not given us a spirit of fear, but of power and of love and of a sound mind" (2 Timothy 1:7). Flood (name of child) with Your love and wash away all fear and doubt. Give her (him) a sense of Your loving presence that far outweighs any fear that would threaten to overtake her (him). Help her (him) to rely on Your power in such a manner that it establishes strong confidence and faith in You.

Prayer Journal

...wash away all fear and doubt

Whenever I am afraid, I will trust in You. In God (I will praise His word), in God I have put my trust; I will not fear.

—PSALM 56:3-4

Lord, help (name of child) not to deny her (his) fears, but take them to You in prayer and seek deliverance from them. I pray that as she (he) draws close to You, Your love will penetrate her (his) life and crowd out all fear. Plant Your Word in her (his) heart. Let faith take root in her (his) mind and soul as she (he) grows in Your Word.

Prayer Journal

...I will trust in You

Do not be conformed to this world, but be transformed by the renewing of your mind, that you may prove what is the good and acceptable and perfect will of God.

—ROMANS 12:2

Lord, please give (name of child) the ability to make clear decisions, to understand all he (she) needs to know, and to be able to focus on what he (she) needs to do. You have said, "You will keep him in perfect peace, whose mind is stayed on You, because he trusts in You" (Isaiah 26:3). I pray that his (her) mind will always be clear, alert, bright, intelligent, stable, peaceful, and uncluttered.

Prayer Journal

Prayer Journal

...whose mind is stayed on You

You shall go out with joy, and be led out with peace; the mountains and the hills shall break forth into singing before you, and all the trees of the field shall clap their hands.

—Isaiah 55:12

Lord, let the spirit of joy rise up in my child's heart this day and may she (he) know the fullness of joy that is found only in Your presence. Whenever she (he) is overtaken by negative emotions, surround her (him) with Your love. Teach her (him) to say, "This is the day that the Lord has made, we will rejoice and be glad in it" (Psalm 118:24).

Prayer Journal

He will yet fill your mouth with laughing, and your lips with rejoicing.

—JOB 8:21

Lord, may negative attitudes have no place in (name of child), nor be a lasting part of her (his) life. May she (he) decide in her (his) heart, "My soul shall be joyful in the LORD; it shall rejoice in His salvation" (Psalm 35:9). Plant Your Word firmly in her (his) heart and increase her (his) faith daily. Enable her (him) to abide in Your love and derive strength from the joy of the Lord this day and forever.

Prayer Journal

The LORD *knows the days of the upright, and their inheritance shall be forever.*

—PSALM 37:18

Lord, You have said in Your Word that a good man leaves an inheritance to his children's children (Proverbs 13:22). I pray that the inheritance I leave to my children will be the rewards of a godly life and a clean heart before You. I also pray that my son (daughter) will "inherit the kingdom prepared for him [her] from the foundation of the world" (Matthew 25:34).

Prayer Journal

Prayer Journal

…their inheritance shall be forever

You have also given me the shield of Your salvation; Your right hand has held me up, Your gentleness has made me great. You enlarged my path under me, so my feet did not slip.

—PSALM 18:35-36

Lord, regarding alcohol and drugs, please make (name of child) strong in You. Draw her (him) close and enable her (him) to put You in control of her (his) life. Speak to her (his) heart, show her (him) the path she (he) should walk, and help her (him) see that protecting her (his) body from things that could destroy it is a part of her (his) service to You.

Prayer Journal

...enlarge my child's path

Whom have I in heaven but You? And there
is none upon earth that I desire besides You.
My flesh and my heart fail; but God is the
strength of my heart and my portion forever.

—PSALM 73:25-26

Lord, Your Word says, "There is a way that
seems right to a man, but its end is the way
of death" (Proverbs 16:25). Give (name of
child) discernment and strength to be able
to say no to things that bring death and yes
to the things of God that bring life. Enable
her (him) to choose life in whatever she (he)
does.

Prayer Journal

...choose life

The body is not for sexual immorality but for the Lord, and the Lord for the body.

—1 CORINTHIANS 6:13

Lord, in the area of sexual purity, please give (name of child) a heart that wants to do what's right in this area, and let purity take root in his (her) personality and guide his (her) actions. Help him (her) to always lay down godly rules for relationships and resist anything that is not Your best. May he (she) long for *Your* approval, Lord, and not allow sexual sin in his (her) life at any time.

Prayer Journal

Prayer Journal

...let purity take root

No temptation has overtaken you except such
as is common to man; but God is faithful,
who will not allow you to be tempted beyond
what you are able, but with the temptation
will also make the way of escape, that you
may be able to bear it.

—1 CORINTHIANS 10:13

Lord, Your Word says, "Blessed is the man
who endures temptation; for when he has
been approved, he will receive the crown of
life which the Lord has promised to those
who love Him" (James 1:12). Make (name
of child) strong enough in You to stand for
what's right and say "No" to sexual
immorality. May Your grace enable him
(her) to be committed to staying pure so
that he (she) will receive Your crown of life.

Prayer Journal

The Power of a Praying Parent

...stand for what's right

Houses and riches are an inheritance from
fathers, but a prudent wife is from the LORD.

—PROVERBS 19:14

Lord, if it's Your will that my child should
marry, send the right husband (wife) at the
perfect time, and give (name of child) a clear
leading from You as to who it is. I pray that
person will be a godly and devoted servant
of Yours, who loves You and lives Your
way, and will be like a son (daughter) to me
and a blessing to all other family members.

Prayer Journal

_____
_____
_____
_____
_____
_____
_____
_____
_____
_____
_____
_____
_____
_____
_____
_____
_____
_____
_____
_____
_____
_____
_____
_____

...send the right one

*From the beginning of the creation, God
made them male and female. For this reason a
man shall leave his father and mother and be
joined to his wife, and the two shall become
one flesh; so then they are no longer two, but
one flesh. Therefore what God has joined
together, let not man separate.*

—MARK 10:6-9

Lord, help my daughter (my son) to know
the difference between simply falling in love
and knowing for certain this is the person
with whom You want her (him) to spend
the rest of her (his) life. May she (he) have
one mate for life, who is also her (his) clos-
est friend. May they be mutually loyal, compassionate, considerate, sensitive, respectful,
affectionate, forgiving, supportive, caring,
and loving toward one another all the days
of their lives.

Prayer Journal

The discretion of a man makes him slow to anger, and it is to his glory to overlook a transgression.

—Proverbs 19:11

Lord, teach (name of child) the depth of Your forgiveness toward him (her) so that he (she) can be freely forgiving toward others. Help him (her) to make the decision to forgive based on what You've asked us to do and not on what feels good at the moment. May he (she) understand that forgiveness doesn't justify the other person's actions; instead, it makes him (her) *free*.

Prayer Journal

Prayer Journal

...be freely forgiving

Let the wicked forsake his way, and the unrighteous man his thoughts; let him return to the Lord, and He will have mercy on him; and to our God, for He will abundantly pardon.

—ISAIAH 55:7

Lord, give (name of child) a heart that is quick to confess her (his) mistakes. May she (he) be truly repentant of them so that she (he) can be forgiven and cleansed. Give her (him) the desire to live in truth before You, and may she (he) say as David did, "Create in me a clean heart, O God, and renew a steadfast spirit within me" (Psalm 51:10).

Prayer Journal

The Power of a Praying Parent

Prayer Journal

...forgiven and cleansed

Repent therefore and be converted, that your sins may be blotted out, so that times of refreshing may come from the presence of the Lord.

—Acts 3:19

Lord, I pray that my daughter (son) will never be able to contain sin within her (him), but rather let there be a longing to confess fully and say, "See if there is any wicked way in me, and lead me in the way everlasting" (Psalm 139:24). May she (he) not live in guilt and condemnation, but rather dwell with a clear conscience in the full understanding of her (his) forgiveness in Christ.

Prayer Journal

Prayer Journal

...dwell with a clear conscience

Though they join forces, the wicked will not go unpunished; but the posterity of the righteous will be delivered.

—PROVERBS 11:21

Lord, I come to You on behalf of (name of child) and ask that You would deliver him (her) from any ungodliness that may be threatening to become a stronghold in his (her) life. Even though I don't know what he (she) needs to be set free from, You do. I pray in the name of Jesus that You will work deliverance in his (her) life wherever it is needed.

Prayer Journal

_..._ *You will work deliverance*

When wisdom enters your heart, and knowl-
edge is pleasant to your soul, discretion will
preserve you, understanding will keep you.

—PROVERBS 2:10-11

Lord, I know that much of my child's happiness in life depends on gaining wisdom and
discernment, which Your Word says brings
long life, wealth, recognition, protection,
enjoyment, contentment, and happiness. I
want all those things for her (him), but I
want them to come as blessings from You.
As she (he) seeks wisdom and discernment
from You, Lord, pour it liberally upon her
(him) so that all her (his) paths will be peace
and life.

Prayer Journal

...seek wisdom and discernment

We are bound to thank God always for you, brethren, as it is fitting, because your faith grows exceedingly, and the love of every one of you all abounds toward each other.

—2 Thessalonians 1:3

Lord, I pray that You would take the faith You have planted in (name of child) and multiply it. May the truth of Your Word be firmly established in his (her) heart so that faith will grow daily and navigate his (her) life. Help him (her) to trust You at all times as he (she) looks to You for truth, guidance, and transformation into Your likeness.

*Therefore, having been justified by faith, we
have peace with God through our Lord Jesus
Christ, through whom also we have access by
faith into this grace in which we stand, and
rejoice in hope of the glory of God.*

—ROMANS 5:1-3

Lord, may (name of child) have a relationship with You that is truly his (her) own—
not an extension of mine or anyone else's. I
want the comfort of knowing that when I'm
no longer on this earth, his (her) faith will
be strong enough to keep him (her) "steadfast, immovable, always abounding in the
work of the Lord" (1 Corinthians 15:58). In
Jesus' name, I pray all of these things.

...faith will grow daily

Prayer Journal